CW01512620

Original title:

Flecked Holes Under the Unicorn Hasp

Copyright © 2025 Swan Charm

Author: Eliora Lumiste

ISBN HARDBACK: 978-1-80563-144-6

ISBN PAPERBACK: 978-1-80564-665-5

Enigmatic Portals of Light

Beyond the veil where shadows dance,
A whispering air, a dream's expanse.
Glimmers flicker, secrets unfold,
In realms of magic, shadows bold.

Gates that shimmer in twilight's hue,
Calling the brave, the hearts so true.
Through the light, the path untwines,
To worlds where time in silence shines.

Mystic runes on ancient stone,
Guarding truths we seek, alone.
Veils as thin as gossamer threads,
Where every step, a fate that treads.

In silence whispered, stars align,
Fingers trace the signs divine.
Portals gleam with promise bright,
Enticing souls to chase the light.

Courage forged in hopes reborn,
Amidst the shadows, dreams are worn.
Each step a choice, a fate's embrace,
In portals bright, we find our place.

Chasing Echoes of Myth

Through verdant glades where legends sigh,
The echoes call, a soft reply.
Footsteps lead where stories weave,
In whispered tales, we dare believe.

Beside the brook where fairies play,
Mythic silhouettes fade away.
Chasing shadows in twilight's hold,
The warmth of narratives yet untold.

On winds of lore, old voices rise,
Crafting truths beneath the skies.
A flicker of magic, a soft refrain,
Reminding us of joy and pain.

In the forest deep, where secrets sleep,
The whispers guard what we shall keep.
In echoes of the past, we find,
A tapestry of hearts entwined.

Rise, dear seeker, to realms unknown,
Let the threads of destiny be sown.
For in each echo of the night,
A trace of magic calls to light.

Cracks of Enchantment Beneath

In the silence, a secret waits,
Beneath the surface, life elates.
Cracks of charm in cobblestone,
Whisper dreams that stand alone.

A flicker here, a laughter there,
Softly woven in the air.
Beneath our feet, the worlds conspire,
Sparkling threads of ancient fire.

In twilight's glow, where shadows play,
The magic lives, though tucked away.
A glimmer of hope, an unexpected greet,
In the hidden folds of time's heartbeat.

With every step, the ground may sigh,
Echoes of spells, both low and high.
Enchantment lives in moments fleet,
Nestled snug in the world's heartbeat.

So tread with care on mystical ground,
For hidden wonders may abound.
In every crack, a joy, a fawn,
Awaits the seeker at each dawn.

Luminous Fragments of Memory

Fleeting moments, a dance of light,
Shimmering echoes of day and night.
Fragments glisten, soft and bright,
In heart's embrace, they take their flight.

Memories woven, a silken thread,
Carried softly where dreams are led.
In twilight's arms, we linger still,
Grasping softly the past's sweet thrill.

With every heartbeat, a story shared,
In radiant whispers, love declared.
Flecks of joy like stars on high,
Guiding us through the woven sky.

Each luminous shard, a tale to tell,
Of laughter sweet and sorrows swell.
As time unfurls its gentle map,
In every fragment, a soft clap.

So treasure these moments, hold them near,
For in their glow, the heart draws near.
In luminous paths of dreams we find,
The sweetest echoes of heart and mind.

Riddles Woven in Stardust

In twilight's embrace, secrets dance,
Whispers of cosmos, a fleeting glance.
Stars twinkle softly, shadows sigh,
Mysteries stir as night draws nigh.

The moon's silver gaze, a riddle spun,
Casting long tales of what's become.
A tapestry woven from dreams so bright,
Guiding lost souls through the velvet night.

With every flicker, a thought takes flight,
Unraveling threads, a curious sight.
Eager hearts chase the fading glow,
In the depths of stardust, truths bestow.

The cosmos murmurs, a cryptic tune,
Hope interlaced, like the light of noon.
In the silence where secrets play,
Riddles await at the end of day.

So listen closely, beyond the veil,
Follow the riddles like a magic trail.
For when the dawn breaks, the answers gleam,
Woven in stardust, a lingering dream.

Dappled Dreams of Illusion

Underneath the boughs where shadows creep,
Lies a realm where dappled dreams seep.
Illusions flutter, like leaves in air,
A dance of wonder, light as a prayer.

In the glimmering mist, figures sway,
Chasing the embers of fading day.
Stories stitched in a fabric of light,
Binding the day to the cool of night.

Each whispered promise, a flickering spark,
Guides the wanderers through the dark.
Through the tangled paths of hearts entwined,
Dappled dreams linger, gracefully aligned.

With every gaze, the world may shift,
Reality bends, like a timeless gift.
In this realm where mirages bloom,
Hope and magic dissolve all gloom.

So dive into dreams where illusions play,
In the land of shadows, let hopes stay.
For there in the whispers, life finds its theme,
In dappled reflections, wakeful dreams.

The Light Behind the Broken Gate

Beyond the threshold of whispered fears,
Lies a realm untouched by time's slow gears.
A broken gate, with stories untold,
Hides treasures gleaming, glistening gold.

Overgrown vines twist in wild embrace,
Yet the light spills forth, a warm, soft grace.
Ancient secrets lie beneath the dust,
In the heart of shadow, we dream and trust.

The echoes of laughter drift through the cracks,
Yearning to bridge the forgotten tracks.
Each step reveals a path of delight,
Leading the lost towards the light.

In this haven, where spirits sing,
Hope reels in joy on ethereal wings.
With every glimpse, the world transforms,
As the light ignites and the heart warms.

So lift your gaze to the horizon's seam,
Discover the magic within each beam.
For behind the gate, life finds its fate,
Embracing the light, we eagerly await.

Mirth in the Corners of Night

In the quiet corners where shadows play,
Lies a hidden laughter, softly at bay.
Mirth in the night, as stars twinkle bright,
Glimmers of joy take graceful flight.

With each gentle breeze that rustles the leaves,
A symphony whispers what the heart believes.
In twilight's embrace, all sorrows cease,
Finding solace in giggles of peace.

Moonlight spills secrets on cobblestone streets,
Casting the stories where laughter repeats.
Children of twilight, they run and they twirl,
Spinning tales woven in starlit whirl.

Here in the darkness, dreams come alive,
Each corner a canvas where hopes can thrive.
With echoes of giggles, the night's alive,
In mirthful moments, our spirits revive.

So dance through the twilight, embrace the delight,
For in every shadow, the heart finds its light.
In laughter resounding, we conquer the night,
Welcoming joy in the soft silver light.

The Lanterns of Infinite Possibility

In twilight's embrace, they softly glow,
Whispers of hope in the night's gentle flow.
Each flicker a choice, a path yet unknown,
Guiding lost souls to the dreams they have sown.

With every step taken, new visions arise,
An infinite canvas beneath starlit skies.
They dance in the darkness, a firefly's flight,
Illuminating futures wrapped in pure light.

Beneath ancient boughs, where secrets reside,
The lanterns beckon, a soft, soothing guide.
Every heart stirred by their flickering flame,
A promise of change whispered tenderly name.

So follow their lead, let your spirit take wing,
Embrace the unknown, for the joy it can bring.
In the lanterns' glow, find your soul's sweet refrain,
A journey of wonder, where love conquers pain.

As night yields to dawn, their light starts to fade,
Yet memories linger, the journeys we've made.
For in every shadow, a spark softly lies,
The lanterns of hope, forever will rise.

Surfaces of Illusion in the Void

Through veils of silence, the echoes swirl,
A tapestry woven where wonders unfurl.
Illusions reflect on the glassy, still streams,
Dancing like shadows through the fabric of dreams.

In corners of thought, where reality bends,
The surface breaks open, where the mind transcends.
Mirages of truth in the whispers of night,
Shimmering fragments, elusive, yet bright.

What limits and bounds shall we choose to defy,
When deep in the void, we dare seek the sky?
The surface can shift, and the landscape can change,
Unlocking a world that feels hauntingly strange.

With each fleeting glance, every form that we chase,
There lies a reflection of the human race.
In strangers and shadows, the beauty, we find,
Surfaces of illusion can reshape the mind.

So dance on the edge where perception runs wild,
Where the void is a canvas, and we are the child.
In the heart of the dark, let your spirit explore,
For in every illusion, there's always much more.

The Allure of Hidden Horizons

Beyond every sunrise, beneath every moon,
Lies a world of secrets that beckons us soon.
With horizons aglow, whispering soft dreams,
The land of the lost, where nothing's as it seems.

In valleys of mystery, the shadows entwine,
Where aspirations linger, and souls intertwine.
A glimpse through the mist, a shiver of chance,
The allure of hidden paths invites us to dance.

Through fields of enchantment, we wander and roam,
Each horizon a promise, a place we call home.
The flutter of wings as the evening draws near,
Guiding our hearts, as the sky becomes clear.

What treasures lie waiting, concealed from our sight,
Draw forth every moment, embrace the twilight.
For with every horizon, a story's unfurled,
In the allure of the hidden, a brand new world.

So venture to places where wonders reside,
Hold tight to your dreams, let your spirit be guide.
For in searching through shadows, the light will appear,
An uncharted horizon, where all becomes clear.

Remnants of a Celestial Convergence

In twilight's embrace, the cosmos will sigh,
As stars sprinkle wishes across velvet sky.
The remnants of light from long distances flown,
Gather like whispers, where all hope is sown.

Each shimmer a secret, a story untold,
Of galaxies waltzing in tapestries bold.
When comets collide, their essence remains,
A dance of the heavens, an echo of rains.

From nebula's cradle to black holes' sweet song,
The universe hums its profound, timeless throng.
Our hearts are the spires, reaching up to the night,
Seizing the magic, the remnants, the light.

In corners of night, where stardust will weep,
The memories linger, celestial deep.
Past worlds, past our own, every dream intertwined,
The convergence of souls, where love is confined.

A tapestry woven through time's endless flow,
The remnants of starlight begin to bestow.
In quiet reflection, the universe knows,
That through every ending, a new journey grows.

Chimeras of Starlit Portals

In shadows where dreams softly weave,
Chimeras dance, where few believe.
Portals flicker, a shimmering gaze,
Inviting the heart to wander and blaze.

In twilight's hush, a whisper calls,
Through ancient woods where the starlight falls.
Mysteries deep in the night's embrace,
Boundless journeys in ethereal space.

A strand of magic, a shimmer of fate,
Each moment a choice to create or negate.
With every step, the cosmos hums,
And in that symphony, the wonder comes.

Visions etched in celestial light,
Awakening dreams that take graceful flight.
Connected by threads that shimmer and shine,
Weaving the timeless with worlds so divine.

So close your eyes and let spirits soar,
For chimeras await on the starlit shore.
With courage, embrace what the heavens start,
And find the enchanted deep in your heart.

Beyond the Canvas of Forgetting

In a realm where memories softly lay,
Brush strokes linger, fading to gray.
Beyond the canvas, stories reside,
Whispers of eras that magic couldn't hide.

Each color a tale, each shade a song,
Echoes of laughter where we once belonged.
The past entwines in layers profound,
In silence, forgotten, such treasures are found.

Yet with every dawn, the world renews,
And paints our visions with vibrant hues.
The heart remembers what time tries to veil,
In dreams, it beckons—an enchanting trail.

Layers of life, like petals unfold,
Each moment a canvas, a story retold.
Brushes of fate, with strokes interlace,
Creating a masterpiece in time and space.

So seek the forgotten, the tales yet to share,
Beyond the canvas, find magic laid bare.
For in every heartbeat, each thread we spill,
Lives the art of existence, the pulse, the thrill.

Flickers of Magic in the Mundane

In every corner, a secret does dwell,
Flickers of magic, like stories to tell.
In the rustle of leaves or a candle's gleam,
The ordinary dances, igniting a dream.

Underneath sighs of the passing day,
A glimmering whisper, in shadows at play.
Teacups of wonder, and smiles that ignite,
Exchange of a glance can shine through the night.

The creak of the floor, the wind through the trees,
Beneath every moment, adventure can tease.
For magic is woven in fabric so fine,
A thread in the heart—a mystical line.

So peel back the layers and open your mind,
For wonder is not just what's grandly designed.
It's in splattered paint, on a forgotten wall,
In laughter of children, where enchantments call.

So take a deep breath, let your spirit roam,
Find flickers of magic wherever you comb.
In the mundane, let the extraordinary gleam,
For life is a tapestry woven with dreams.

The Glow Beyond the Fringes

Beneath the twilight, the world holds its breath,
A glow on the fringes, where shadows bequeath.
The light dances softly, with secrets to share,
As whispers of starlight drift sweetly through air.

In the heart of the night, where wonders convene,
A vision of magic, like threads in between.
Look closely, dear seeker, at what lies ahead,
For flickers of fortune are easily bred.

Through branches and twilight, where dreams intertwine,
Flashes of brilliance, like wine on the vine.
Each glimmer a promise, each shimmer a guide,
In the glow beyond fringes, let your heart slide.

With each gentle pulse of the advancing night,
Adventure awaits in the margins of light.
So tread with intention on paths unseen,
Discover the beauty in realms in between.

Embrace the unknown, let curiosity flow,
For life is more vibrant where possibilities grow.
In the glow beyond fringes, your spirit will soar,
Where dreams become real and unite evermore.

Flickering Portals in Dreamscapes

In shadows deep where whispers play,
A flickering light guides the way.
Through shimmering doors of silken thread,
Where dreams are spun and softly said.

In twilight's grasp, the colors swirl,
As secrets dance, and visions twirl.
A fleeting glimpse of worlds unknown,
Within the heart, the seeds have grown.

The softly flaring, distant beams,
Invite us forth to weave our dreams.
With every step, the silence sighs,
Revealing truth in skyscape lies.

Through each portal, a story found,
In ravishing realms, we're tightly bound.
As echoes linger, softly sweet,
In kindred hearts, our fates will meet.

So chase the flickers, heed their call,
In dreamscapes vast, we learn to fall.
With every heartbeat, let us dare,
To soar through shadows, light the air.

Twinkling Secrets of the Mystic Clasp

In secret glades where moonbeams glance,
The clasp of fate begins to dance.
With twinkling secrets hidden deep,
In mysteries that softly creep.

Each shimmer holds a tale untold,
Of hidden paths in realms of gold.
A whispered wish upon the breeze,
Unlocks a world of sweet reprise.

The core of magic lies concealed,
In treasures lost, in dreams revealed.
A clasp that binds the heart so tight,
Holds every hope within its light.

As starlit skies beckon the night,
We grasp the clasp and take our flight.
With every twinkle, joy expands,
In the embrace of gentle hands.

So wander forth on paths unknown,
With twinkling secrets fully grown.
Embrace the quiet, trust your heart,
For every clasp is just the start.

Lace Patterns on the Horizon of Wonder

Upon the horizon, lace is sewn,
With threads of magic, softly blown.
In patterns bright, the sunbeams weave,
A tapestry for those who believe.

As day unfolds, a gleaming sight,
The dance of dreams in morning light.
With each new dawn, the wonders call,
Whispering hope through ethereal hall.

The edges curl with misty grace,
In every corner, a hidden place.
Where laughter sparkles, shadows play,
And hearts embrace the light of day.

With lace entwined in nature's art,
Exploring realms that fill the heart.
Our spirits rise on wings of air,
As wonders bloom everywhere.

So walk with me, where dreams unfurl,
On horizons bold, a magic swirl.
In every stitch, a story spun,
Together, we will greet the sun.

Twilit Whispers Beneath the Gleaming Hug

In twilight's hue, where shadows blend,
Whispers echo, a soothing friend.
Beneath the stars, a gleaming hug,
Embracing all in night's soft tug.

The moonlit path is gently traced,
In silken threads, our fears displaced.
With every whisper, courage grows,
As hopes unfurl like blooming rose.

The night unveils its velvet charm,
A tender warmth, a sweet alarm.
We speak in tones of trust and grace,
In this embraced, enchanted space.

As shadows weave with silver light,
We share our secrets deep in night.
Each twilit breath a promise made,
In gleaming hugs, our naiveté.

So linger here, where dreams unite,
In whispers soft, we'll take our flight.
With every hug, the world feels right,
In twilit realms, we ignite the night.

Shimmering Pauses in Fantastical Journeys

In forests deep where shadows loom,
The whispers call beneath the gloom.
Each step a dance on mossy floor,
A world awaits, forevermore.

With every breath the magic swells,
A spark ignites where silence dwells.
The winding paths of dreams untold,
Lead hearts to wonders, brave and bold.

The moonlight weaves a shimmering thread,
Through tangled tales of those who tread.
In swirling mists, the spirits play,
Guiding lost souls along the way.

In twilight's arms, the colors blend,
Each pause a note, a journey's end.
A fleeting glance, a tender sigh,
Where hopes take flight and fears comply.

So tread with care on colors bright,
For every pause can spark delight.
In fantastical realms where dreams align,
The shimmering pauses intertwine.

Twisted Ribbons of Celestial Light

In midnight skies where starlight weaves,
Twisted ribbons dance like leaves.
Each swirl a tale of ancient grace,
A woven dream in cosmic space.

They shimmer soft, in silence rare,
With echoes of a love laid bare.
Upon the breeze, they sway and spin,
Unraveling secrets held within.

The galaxies hum a soothing song,
Whilst ribbons twist where souls belong.
A tapestry of life afloat,
In every hue, we find our coat.

They guide us through the darkened night,
Illuminating paths so bright.
In every turn, a glance divine,
A cosmic dance, a fate enshrined.

So heed the call of distant stars,
For twisted ribbons bear no scars.
Embrace the light, let spirits soar,
In celestial bonds, forevermore.

Veiled Secrets in the Fabric of Time

Within the folds of time's embrace,
Lie hidden truths that leave no trace.
Each whisper cloaked in shadows deep,
A promise made, a secret keep.

The threads of fate entwine and weave,
In patterns only dreams perceive.
As moments drift like autumn leaves,
We chase the past, though it deceives.

The ticking clock, a rhythmic dance,
Unravels dreams with every chance.
In stillness lies the key to find,
The veiled secrets, intertwined.

With every breath, the echoes fade,
In time's embrace, the light is laid.
A journey through the when and where,
To meet the hearts that linger there.

So sail upon the winds of change,
Through spaces wide and voices strange.
Embrace the veils that time has sewn,
In fabric spun, our truths are grown.

Sparkling Glades of Hidden Wonders

In glades where sunlight softly gleams,
Hidden wonders weave through dreams.
A dance of petals on the breeze,
Where laughter sings and troubles ease.

The forest hums a gentle tune,
Beneath the watchful, silver moon.
Each nook a stage where fairies play,
In harmony, they greet the day.

At twilight's fall, the magic swells,
With whispered hopes and secret spells.
In every corner, treasures bloom,
A sparkling light dispels the gloom.

The brooklet laughs, the leaves do sway,
In sparkling glades, we laugh and play.
Each moment holds a world anew,
With hidden wonders, bold and true.

So wander forth with open heart,
In nature's arms, let dreams depart.
For every glade holds joys to find,
In sparkling realms, skip doubts behind.

Intricate Designs of Enchantment

In shadows deep where whispers weave,
The threads of magic gently cleave.
Each pattern drawn, a secret told,
A tapestry of dreams unfold.

With wands that flicker like a flame,
We dance within the arcane frame.
With olden runes and potions brewed,
The air is thick with hope renewed.

Upon the parchment, ink will flow,
Beneath the stars, our passions glow.
With every symbol, lives entwine,
A world reborn through hands divine.

The moonlight whispers ancient spells,
In every heart, a wish that dwells.
From dreamers' souls, the magic sends,
Enchantment weaves, and never ends.

Through corridors of time we race,
Bound by the charm of fate's embrace.
Together drawn, our spirits thrive,
In intricate designs, we're alive.

Fragments of a Celestial Dance

In swirling skies where starlight streams,
The galaxies spin in whispered dreams.
Each twinkle holds a story bright,
A dance of shadows caught in light.

With comet tails that brush the night,
We grasp at wonders, infinite flight.
The heavens sing a lullaby,
While planets weave a silent sigh.

From distant worlds, the echoes call,
As nebulas in splendor fall.
Fragments of fate in cosmic trance,
We twirl through time, a fleeting glance.

With every step, the stars align,
In cosmic patterns, hearts combine.
A choreography of the bold,
In fragments, let our tales be told.

So let us soar on wings of fate,
Embrace the dance, don't hesitate.
For in this realm, we shall expand,
In fragments bright, we take our stand.

Dimensional Rifts of Magic

Through portals bright that beckon wide,
We step beyond our worlds of pride.
A tapestry of realms await,
In rifts where fate and magic mate.

With whispered charms on winds that tease,
Secrets flow like autumn leaves.
Each world a mirror, each glance a clue,
To mysteries hidden just for you.

In shadows deep, where echoes dwell,
We weave our dreams and cast a spell.
With every shard of light we see,
The rifts in time, our destiny.

An astral map, a starry guide,
With open hearts, we shall not hide.
In every clash of realms untold,
Our magic shines, both fierce and bold.

For through the rifts, we shall explore,
The depths of magic evermore.
Each journey wide, a truth to gift,
In dimensional rifts, our spirits lift.

The Stillness Beyond the Luminescence

In quiet voids where silence reigns,
The whispers of the night remain.
Beyond the glow of dawn's embrace,
A stillness waits, a sacred space.

With shadows draped on tranquil shores,
Mysteries hide behind closed doors.
In peace we find a gentle balm,
The quiet breath of nature's calm.

Where light entwines with dusk's retreat,
And time stands still beneath our feet.
In stillness, hearts can hear the call,
Of universe, embracing all.

With eyes closed tight, we seek the light,
In moments pure, where souls take flight.
The luminescence fades away,
In stillness, dreams begin to play.

So linger here, where echoes fade,
In quietude, our fears allayed.
For in the hush, we find our grace,
The stillness grants a timeless space.

Twilight's Laughter in the Gloom

In shadows where the soft winds sigh,
Twilight weaves a gentle cry.
The stars begin their playful dance,
While dreams ignite from a single glance.

Laughter echoes through the night,
A flicker of magic in fading light.
The moonbeams tease with silvery gleam,
Drawing forth the heart's secret dream.

Whispers linger on the cool breeze,
As time slows down, inviting ease.
In twilight's arms, the world takes flight,
Lost in the wonder of brief twilight.

With every sparkle, a tale unfolds,
Of forgotten adventures, brave and bold.
Through veils of dusk, our spirits rise,
Chasing the laughter beneath the skies.

Embracing the night with open hearts,
In every shadow, a tale imparts.
Twilight's laughter, forever it blooms,
Lighting our paths through the gathering glooms.

Celestial Whispers of the Unknown

In the silence where the galaxies spin,
Celestial secrets begin to grin.
Stars like lanterns guide our way,
Through the mysteries of night and day.

Whispers of old in the cosmic sea,
Speak softly to those who dare to see.
Each twinkle holds stories untold,
In shimmering dust, the universe unfolds.

Planets waltz in their luminous trance,
Inviting the dreamers to join the dance.
Time drips like honey, sweet and slow,
In the realm of magic where wonders grow.

Voices echo from distant skies,
Inviting our hearts to dream and rise.
The unknown glimmers with each breath,
A promise of life, a taste of death.

As we gaze into the endless night,
We find our dreams taking flight.
In every spark, a promise rests,
A celestial journey, a heartfelt quest.

A Mosaic of Dreams and Mysteries

In a tapestry spun from whispered sighs,
Dreams weave together beneath soft skies.
Colors collide in the starlit night,
Forming a mosaic of pure delight.

Each shard a memory, a tale once bright,
Echoes of laughter, whispers of fright.
Within each fragment, a spark of magic,
Reflecting the heart, both joyous and tragic.

Through the shadows where secrets play,
We gather the fragments, come what may.
Every dream a path, every mystery a key,
Unlocking the wonders of who we can be.

In every heart lies a story untold,
Yearning to shine, brave and bold.
Together we weave, together we mend,
A mosaic of dreams that never shall end.

With threads of hope and ties of fate,
We dance through the night, awake, never late.
In the whispers of dawn, our dreams intertwine,
Painting the world with a magic divine.

Kaleidoscope of Forgotten Fables

In a kaleidoscope spun with forgotten lore,
Fables arise from the ocean's roar.
Colors collide in vibrant display,
Inviting the heart on a whimsical sway.

Once upon a time, the stories would sing,
Of dragons and giants with delicate wings.
Each twist reveals a new shift in time,
Echoes of legends in meter and rhyme.

Through shadows of memory, we wander and roam,
Unraveling tales that once felt like home.
In every corner, a story holds sway,
Fables forgotten, yet here they stay.

Magic lingers like dew on the grass,
Kaleidoscopic dreams that eternally pass.
Unravel the threads and breathe in their grace,
Find the forgotten in our timeless embrace.

Bound by the stories we dare to reclaim,
In the heart of the night, we gather their names.
In whispers, they dance; in shadows, they play,
A kaleidoscope of fables forever will stay.

Mysterious Pathways of the Night

Beneath the stars that softly glow,
Shadows dance where moonlight flows.
Whispers travel on the breeze,
Secrets wrap 'round ancient trees.

Mist swirls gently, cloaking the ground,
Every sound, a mystic sound.
Footsteps echo, fading light,
Illuminating paths of night.

Through the foliage, spirits glide,
Guardians of this twilight tide.
In their gaze, the world seems strange,
Every corner knows a change.

Delicate webs of silver thread,
Draw you close, yet fill with dread.
In the quiet, truths unfold,
Tales from ages long since told.

With every turn and every stair,
Mysterious sights await you there.
Light the lantern, herald the dawn,
For once the night's charm is gone.

Secrets Layered in Celestial Flickers

Stars ignite the velvet sky,
Whispers of the cosmos high.
Every flicker tells a tale,
Of lost loves and ships that sail.

Layered dreams in silken night,
Glimmer faint, yet ever bright.
Constellations softly cry,
Mapping paths where wishes lie.

In the dance of ancient orbs,
Timeless secrets, fate absorbs.
Chasing echoes of the past,
Holding memories that can't last.

Moonbeams twine with dew-laden grass,
Moments fleeting, yet they pass.
Gaze away, but don't forget,
The depth of every twilight threat.

As the night reveals its heart,
Every shimmer plays its part.
Secrets beckon, softly sown,
In the depths of stars alone.

Unraveling the Threads of Daydreams

In a realm where visions swirl,
Daydreams drift and gently twirl.
Threads of thought begin to weave,
Tapestries of hearts believe.

Colors bloom in radiant hues,
Softly whispering hidden clues.
Each intention speaks a song,
In this space where dreams belong.

Untangle moments, let them glide,
Through the corridors inside.
As daylight yields to mystic nights,
The heart uncovers secret sights.

Footsteps echo in the mind,
Fantasies we seek to find.
Winding paths of light and shade,
In the labyrinth we have made.

So close your eyes, embrace the sway,
Journey forth where dreams can play.
For within these threads we chase,
Lie the wonders we embrace.

Surreal Echoes of Twilight Whispers

As twilight kisses day goodbye,
Echoes linger, softly sigh.
Whispers cling to fading light,
Tales unfurl with coming night.

Every shadow holds a voice,
Stirring hearts to make a choice.
In this hush, the world transforms,
Outside stillness, magic swarms.

Crickets serenade the dusk,
Each note rich, with life, and trust.
Surreal scenes, both bright and dark,
Leave a mark, ignite a spark.

Moments blend in twilight's hue,
Painting secrets, pure and true.
Caught between the dusk and dawn,
A tapestry we softly spawn.

Breathe in deeply, feel the calm,
Night's embrace, a gentle balm.
For when whispers fill the air,
Surreal echoes linger there.

Shattered Realities of Fantasia

In lands where shadows softly creep,
Dreamers dance in secrets deep.
A whisper flows through ancient trees,
As magic sways upon the breeze.

Fractured worlds in twilight blend,
Where truths and fables twist and bend.
A portal glimmers, bright and wide,
Inviting souls on daring rides.

Winds of change weave tales untold,
In vibrant hues of brave and bold.
The spirits sigh, their pain laid bare,
In realms that echo every prayer.

Yet hope, a flame that never dies,
Sparks in hearts, igniting skies.
Through shattered glass, we find our way,
In Fantasia, night meets day.

So hold your dreams with tender grace,
For in their light, you'll find your place.
In every shard, a story's cast,
In every breath, the die is cast.

An Odyssey through Hidden Realms

Beyond the hills where sunbeams play,
A path untraveled leads the way.
With every step, the ground will shift,
Each moment offers a strange gift.

The clouds above are painted bright,
As riddles dance in morning light.
A river sings its wild refrain,
Through valleys lush and hills of grain.

A castle looms in misty haze,
Where lost souls wander through the maze.
Each room conceals a tale profound,
A whispered truth in echoes found.

Though shadows loom and doubts arise,
Adventure calls, beneath wide skies.
With courage forged from ancient stone,
An odyssey that leads us home.

So gather heart and take the leap,
Through hidden realms, the brave shall reap.
In every turn, the heart will soar,
For in the quest lies so much more.

Echoes of the Fabled Light

In twilight's grasp, where legends dwell,
A beacon glows, its charm a spell.
Stories weave in threads of gold,
As wonders wait for hearts so bold.

In whispers soft, the echoes play,
Of heroes lost along the way.
Their journeys etched in flame and star,
A memory held both near and far.

Through valleys deep and mountains high,
The fabled light will never die.
It guides the weary through the night,
With every step, it shines so bright.

The shadows stretch, yet hope remains,
In every heart, a spark that reigns.
Bravado kindles dreams anew,
As echoes guide the faithful few.

So seek the light, let not it fade,
In moral tales, the truth is laid.
For in the echoes, we'll find our might,
In fables born of endless light.

Curious Glimmers Beneath the Surface

Down in the depths where shadows dance,
Curious glimmers weave their chance.
A world of secrets, quiet and rare,
Where wonders bloom, in silent air.

Beneath the waves, a song is sung,
Of stories old and hearts so young.
An ocean deep, a realm unexplored,
For every truth, a treasure stored.

With every glance, the surface breaks,
Revealing paths that fate now makes.
The tide pulls forth, then pulls away,
In ebb and flow, we find our way.

Each shimmering spark holds tales of old,
Of magic spun through grains of gold.
And with each breath, the water sways,
The past and present intertwine their ways.

So dive beneath, embrace the thrill,
In every wave, the heart shall fill.
With curious glimmers, bright and bold,
New worlds awaken, stories told.

The Alluring Mystery of Soft Shadows

In dusk's embrace, shadows play,
Whispers of dreams in shades of gray.
Silent secrets they weave and spin,
A tapestry soft, where tales begin.

Through tangled woods, soft echoes dwell,
Each corner turned, a hidden spell.
Timid sparks of light take flight,
Glowing softly through the night.

In every sigh, a story told,
Of timeless wonders, soft and bold.
The shimmer of stars, a lost delight,
Calls out to wanderers in twilight.

Beneath the boughs, old legends sigh,
In murmurs low, where dreams may lie.
The dance of dusk, a waltz divine,
With every flicker, fate aligns.

Come gather near, in the twilight's hold,
Where stories sleep and hearts grow old.
In shadow's fold, we'll find our way,
In softest whispers, where secrets stay.

Secrets that Dance in the Twilight

A twilight breeze whispers low,
Carrying tales of long ago.
In the fading light, spirits twirl,
As the stars above begin to whirl.

Among the trees, the shadows sway,
Holding secrets of the day.
With every rustle, a promise stirs,
In the hushed power of what occurs.

The twilight hour, a magic grace,
Embracing time in a tender place.
Each flicker and gleam, a truth renowned,
In this quiet hour, hope is found.

Hear the whispers of the night,
Echoing wonders, soft and bright.
In every silence, a chance to see,
What lies beneath, what's meant to be.

With every shadow, stories ignite,
In the magical glow of fading light.
Let your heart embrace the chance,
To join the secrets in their dance.

Enchanted Shards of Reality

Beneath the surface, magic glows,
In hidden realms, where no one knows.
Fragments of dreams, like scattered stars,
Reveal the wonders that lie afar.

In crystal pools, reflections gleam,
A reality born of a whispered dream.
Each shard of truth, a path to take,
In the quiet night, where hearts awake.

The normal fades, the mystical calls,
As spells enfold within these walls.
With every glance, the world transforms,
Unraveling mystery, breaking norms.

Dance through the shards, a journey grand,
In a realm where magic takes a stand.
The impossible glimmers in soft light,
Whispers of wonder in the night.

In every glimmer, a story hides,
In the enchanted shards, the spirit bides.
Gather the magic, let it unfold,
For within these pieces, dreams are told.

Beyond the Edge of Known Dreams

Where dreams take flight beyond the veil,
And hopes weave stories we long to tell.
Past twilight's edge, through starlit skies,
A world awakens, hidden from eyes.

In the quiet hush, musings unfold,
With every heartbeat, adventures bold.
Farther and farther, the journey we seek,
Where whispers of magic begin to speak.

With each step forward, a new refrain,
In the realms of wonder, we break the chain.
Endless horizons call out our name,
In the dance of shadows, we play the game.

Embrace the unknown, let courage soar,
For dreams are waiting behind the door.
Beyond the edge of all we know,
Lies a universe where magic flows.

So journey on, past the realms we claim,
In the tapestry rich with love and flame.
For in every heartbeat, a dream resides,
In the land of wonder, where magic abides.

Halos of Hope Between the Cracks

In whispers soft, the shadows dance,
Where light partakes a fleeting glance.
Hope blooms bright in cracks so small,
A guiding spark amid the fall.

With every sigh, new dreams ignite,
Like stars that pierce the velvet night.
In hidden corners, magic stirs,
As fate unveils the world as hers.

Through silent paths where echoes roam,
The heart finds always its true home.
In every fracture, love can weave,
A tapestry of all we believe.

So take my hand, embrace the glow,
We'll chase the light that dares to show.
For halos form from shattered past,
And in our unity, we'll last.

Across the ages, spirits rise,
Reclaiming whispers, softest sighs.
For in the cracks, we find our way,
Through halos forged in bright dismay.

The Dreamwalker's Guiding Light

By moonlit paths, the dreamers tread,
In realms where every wish is fed.
With gentle hands, they weave the night,
A guiding star, a spark of light.

Through clouds of thought, they deftly glide,
With open hearts, and arms spread wide.
Each dream a thread, they twine and spin,
Where loss gives way, and hope begins.

In twilight's calm, the visions soar,
Unlocking secrets, opening doors.
As shadows fade, the truth ignites,
In ether's grasp, they claim their rights.

To walk these halls of future's fate,
Where joy and sorrow intertwine so great.
The dreamwalkers know what must be done,
To coax the dawn, to greet the sun.

And when the world feels lost in gray,
They guide us back to brighter days.
For in their light, we dare to dream,
A tapestry, reality's gleam.

Adrift in a Dreamt Continuum

In currents swift, the dreamers sail,
Where time and space begin to pale.
Through veils of thought, we drift and dive,
In endless realms, we come alive.

Each breath a thread, each heartbeat song,
To worlds unknown where we belong.
In whispers soft, we chase the night,
Adrift in visions, pure delight.

With every turn, a new surprise,
A tapestry of lucid skies.
In waking dreams, we're free to roam,
In stardust paths, we find our home.

So let us dance on moonbeams bright,
Through endless dreams, we'll share the light.
For in this weave of what may be,
Our spirits soar forever free.

And when the dawn begins to break,
We'll hold our dreams, no chance to shake.
In the continuum where we play,
Adrift in magic, come what may.

Serendipity of Shattered Views

In shattered glass, a world anew,
Reflections speak of paths we rue.
With every shard, a story twirls,
Of hidden joys in fractured worlds.

Through twisted sights, we learn to see,
The beauty born from what will be.
In chaos, grace begins to bloom,
As hope emerges from the gloom.

The twists of fate, a dance so sweet,
In serendipity, we find our feet.
For each misstep shapes the way,
A wondrous path to brighter day.

With every tear, a lesson learned,
In shattered views, the heart has yearned.
To see the light in broken seams,
In every fault, there lie our dreams.

So raise a toast to lives askew,
In harmony with each adieu.
For in the cracks, we come to know,
The serendipity of the flow.

Mysteries Woven in Starlight

In the stillness of the night,
Whispers dance in silver light.
Secrets held by moonlit beams,
Stirring softly in our dreams.

Through the shadows, stories creep,
Ancient tales the heavens keep.
Constellations weave and sway,
In the fabric of the gray.

Glimmers echo through the dark,
Each a universe, a spark.
Cosmic wonders softly sigh,
As they trace the velvet sky.

Threads of fate entwined with stars,
Tell of journeys, near and far.
In the silence, truth draws near,
Echoes of a world we hear.

With each blink, a world anew,
Vast horizons crafted blue.
In the heart of night, we find,
Mysteries that bind our mind.

Shadows of the Ethereal Latch

In the corners where night falls,
Ethereal whispers softly call.
Shadows linger, secrets mask,
In their dance, the questions bask.

Doors that open, softly creak,
Paths that promise, yet now seek.
Lurking features, veiled in gray,
Guide the traveler, lost astray.

Each shadow holds a story deep,
Woven in the realms of sleep.
Mysterious shapes glide with ease,
Telling truths like shifting breeze.

Echoes drift through midnight air,
Enigmas spun with utmost care.
A latch that waits, a heart that yearns,
In the dark, the lantern burns.

As the day begins to fare,
Shadows dart with whispers rare.
In their depths, the answers cling,
To the mysteries that they bring.

Splinters of Magic Under Gleaming Rain

Raindrops fall like glassy gems,
Dancing on the window's hems.
Splinters of a world unknown,
Where enchanting dreams are sown.

Each droplet glistens, tells a tale,
Of distant lands where fairies sail.
Underneath the stormy sky,
Magic touches, drifts and sighs.

Puddles ripple with delight,
As secrets surface in the night.
Whispers float on every breeze,
Carrying the hopes of trees.

With every flash of lightning's glare,
Unveils the beauty hidden there.
A realm where wonder intertwines,
And mystery in each heart shines.

So let the rain, sweet magic's tune,
Draw you close beneath the moon.
For in the storm's wild embrace,
Is a splintered, sacred space.

Enchanted Threads of Twilight Tales

As daylight wanes and colors blend,
Twilight weaves where shadows mend.
Stories whisper in the trees,
Carried softly by the breeze.

Threads of magic spin and swirl,
In the hearts of every girl.
Beneath the stars, their voices blend,
In every tale, a secret friend.

The moon, a guardian, stands tall,
Casting light on creatures small.
In her glow, the stories rise,
Colors dancing in the skies.

Each leaf tells of dreams once spun,
In the twilight, we are one.
With every breath, our hopes take flight,
Guided by the fading light.

So gather 'round, let legends flow,
As twilight paints the world below.
In the fabric of the night,
Enchanted threads weave pure delight.

Whispers in Tattered Dreams

In the silence, shadows creep,
Carried forth by winds that weep,
Faded echoes softly hum,
Tales of what will come undone.

Beneath the moon's pale, watchful gaze,
Flickering hopes in twilight's maze,
Each whisper spun from threads of night,
A tapestry of wondrous fright.

Tattered dreams on gentle tides,
Where the heart's true longing hides,
Fleeting moments blend and bend,
In this realm where dreams transcend.

Through the mist, a figure calls,
Softly brushing velvet walls,
With every sigh, they weave a strand,
A magic born from their own hand.

So drift away on feathered wings,
Into the night where starlight sings,
Embrace the shadows, let them in,
For in this world, the dreams begin.

Shadows of Celestial Gaps

Between the stars, a story laid,
In whispers lost, a spirit swayed,
Echoed sighs through cosmic dark,
Finding shape, igniting spark.

Beneath the veil of twilight's grace,
Starlit paths in a boundless space,
Each shadow speaks of tales long past,
And dreams that flew but could not last.

In celestial gaps where secrets dwell,
The nightingale sings its haunting spell,
Carving light through folds of gloom,
As silence breathes within the room.

Tangled in the cosmic thread,
Where wishes whisper, fears misled,
A waltz of shadows, soft and deep,
In spectral realms where secrets seep.

So linger here, lost in the night,
In shadows cast by fading light,
For in the dark, you'll surely find,
The echoes of a dreaming mind.

The Midnight Tapestry of Wonder

In twilight's grasp, the magic weaves,
A midnight cloak that softly leaves,
A tapestry of dreams unfold,
In threads of silver, deep and bold.

Within this realm, where wishes soar,
The heart discovers, yearns for more,
Each stitch a tale of hope and fear,
The fabric sings for those who hear.

Whispers paint the edges bright,
Embroidered hearts in gentle light,
As echoes of forgotten lore,
Awake in stories waiting for.

Stars cascade like drops of dew,
In every wisp, a world anew,
Rest upon this woven grace,
Find your truth in this embrace.

So join the dance of night's delight,
Embrace the magic, take your flight,
For in the midnight's softest hand,
You'll find the dreams forever stand.

Secrets in a Star-Stitched Sky

In the velvet of the night,
Whispers twinkle, soft and bright,
Each star holds a secret deep,
A promise made for those who leap.

In stitched constellations high,
Hidden truths begin to fly,
They cradle dreams in silken light,
In shadows kissed by dawn's first sight.

Listen close to cosmic sighs,
Every flicker, every rise,
In silence, stories bold are spun,
Of journeys shared and battles won.

Through the fabric of the skies,
Awaits the heart that longs and tries,
With every wish upon a light,
The stars will guide through endless night.

So wander forth where wonders gleam,
In the whispers of a dream,
For secrets in this sky of lore,
Awaken souls to seek for more.

The Veil of Ethereal Whimsy

In realms where dreams begin to spin,
A tapestry of light draws in.
With whispers soft as dusk's embrace,
We dance in shadows, time and space.

Beneath the moon's soft, silver gaze,
Magic twirls through hidden maze.
Each laughter bursts like morning dew,
A spark of wonder, bright and new.

The stars conspire to weave their tales,
In glimmers where the silence wails.
A flick of wand, a gaze askew,
The veil reveals what's dark and true.

In corners dim, where hopes will sway,
Ethereal whimsy lights the way.
With every twirl, a secret spun,
In shadows past, the heart's won run.

Through laughter, tears, and endless flight,
We chase the whispers of the night.
And find within the folds of time,
A world where every dream can climb.

Patterns of Starlit Intrigue

Upon the canvas of the night,
Patterns dance, a wondrous sight.
Through velvet skies, the secrets glide,
In cosmic intrigue, hearts collide.

Each star a tale of love and fate,
A twinkle lost, a restless state.
With every brush of silken light,
The universe unveils its might.

Orbs of brilliance weave a web,
From whispered bonds that hearts can ebb.
In silver streams of time, we drift,
As starlit patterns shift and lift.

The cosmos holds its breath each night,
As we unveil its hidden light.
In dreams, we find our stories told,
Through patterns rich and moments bold.

By dawn's first kiss, the tales shall fade,
Yet in our hearts, the magic laid.
We carry forth the starlit song,
Inspires us to journey long.

Echoing in Twilight's Canvas

In twilight's grip, the whispers flow,
An echo stirs where shadows go.
Soft hues of indigo and gold,
Trace stories waiting to be told.

With every brush, the dusk awakes,
In every lull, the silence breaks.
The canvas stretches wide and free,
Reflecting what we yearn to see.

Each heartbeat pulses with the night,
As twilight draws the day's last light.
We weave our hopes in twilight's thread,
Where dreams are born and fears are shed.

Through night's embrace, we drift and soar,
In every echo, seek for more.
The canvas beckons, tales unfold,
In whispers soft and colors bold.

As dawn arrives, the echoes fade,
Yet in our minds, the visions laid.
In twilight's hold, forever glean,
The art of life, both raw and keen.

Gossamer Threads of Imagination

In webs of thought where dreams entwine,
Gossamer threads of pure design.
With every spin, a world takes flight,
In vibrant realms of pure delight.

Through fragile strands, our hopes are cast,
In fantasies, both slow and fast.
Each whisper sung in silken breath,
Breathes life into the dance of death.

Unfolding tales of joy and woe,
In every thread, we learn and grow.
The loom of life spins bright and clear,
An artful tapestry, we steer.

With colors drawn from deep within,
Imagination stirs, begins.
In every knot, a story waits,
To bridge the gap of starlit fates.

So let us weave our dreams with care,
In gossamer threads, find magic there.
For in each twine, a spark ignites,
Creating worlds in countless heights.

Cryptic Threads in Enchanted Realms

In twilight's glow, the secrets weave,
Through shadowed paths where dreams conceive.
A flickering light, a whispered sound,
In thickets deep, lost hopes are found.

The moonlit glow, a silken veil,
Guides wandering hearts on a mystic trail.
With every step, the echoes call,
Of tales once lost, forgotten all.

The stars above, like scattered gold,
Unravel truth from stories old.
A tapestry spun from night's embrace,
Threads of magic in timeless space.

With every turn, a shadow stirs,
A riddle spoken, the silence blurs.
In enchanted realms where spirits play,
The cryptic threads lead us away.

From woven fates, the whispers sigh,
In realms where dreams and legends lie.
So follow the path, let courage rise,
For in the dark, the magic lies.

Ethereal Loops of Whispered Wishes

In circles drawn on moonlit grass,
Wishes dance as moments pass.
Soft-spoken hopes on a fleeting breeze,
Entwined in loops, like whispered trees.

The constellations twinkle bright,
Guardians of secrets held so tight.
Echoes of dreams float through the air,
Carried by starlight, pure and rare.

With every sigh, a wish takes flight,
Turning shadows into light.
In ethereal loops, destiny sways,
Guiding hearts through the darkest days.

In gentle sighs, the night reveals,
Magic sealed in timeless seals.
Whispered charms in the starlit scope,
Are woven with threads of endless hope.

So gather your wishes, let them soar,
In loops of wisdom, forevermore.
For in that dance, the soul shall find,
The ethereal ties that bind mankind.

Charmed Interstices of Midnight's Embrace

In midnight's cloak, the stars align,
Whispers float like aged wine.
Charmed interstices in shadow's glow,
Hold tales untold of ebb and flow.

Through forests deep, where silence breathes,
Ancient secrets hide beneath leaves.
With every rustle, a promise stirs,
In the heart of night, forgotten whirs.

The moon, a guide, with silver light,
Unravels threads in the still of night.
In embraces soft, where shadows quail,
Time weaves its magic, a whispered trail.

The world asleep, but dreams awake,
In charmed interstices, the heart shall ache.
For every wish that dares to rise,
Is wrapped in illusions, shrouded skies.

So listen close to the night's refrain,
In every lull, there's joy and pain.
In midnight's arms, we shall find grace,
In charmed interstices, our own space.

Glinting Canopies of Imagined Worlds

Beneath the stars, the wonders gleam,
Glinting canopies, a dreamer's dream.
Through forests wild, in fields of gold,
Imagination blooms, tales unfold.

Every leaf a story, every sky a verse,
In whispered winds, the stars converse.
With each soft rustle, magic stirs,
In glinting realms, the heart prefers.

The rivers hum a lullaby sweet,
Where shadows dance and silence meets.
In worlds imagined, paths entwine,
With glory found in designs divine.

Through valleys deep, where hopes reside,
The glimmering light becomes our guide.
In canopies wide, the spirit flies,
Embracing freedom beneath the skies.

So wander forth, let dreams unfurl,
In glinting canopies of this vast world.
For in each heartbeat, a world awaits,
In imagined realms, where magic creates.

Beyond the Veil of Starlit Whispers

Beyond the veil where shadows play,
The starlit whispers softly sway.
In twilight's grip, the secrets glide,
As dreams alight on silver tide.

Enchanted tales the night recalls,
With every sigh, the silence falls.
Through sapphire skies, the wishes soar,
A dance of light forevermore.

The moonbeams weave a gentle song,
Where heartbeat rhythms first belong.
In starry halls, the magic lives,
And every wish a heartbeat gives.

As dawn approaches, shadows flee,
In each farewell, there's mystery.
Yet in the breeze, hope lingers near,
For whispers call, they draw us here.

A tapestry of night unfolds,
With stories bright and treasures bold.
Beyond the veil, where dreams await,
The starlit whispers guide our fate.

Reflections of Forgotten Echoes

In quiet rooms where memories lie,
Forgotten echoes start to sigh.
A flickering flame, a shadowed glance,
The past entwined in a wistful dance.

Each reflection holds a tale untold,
Of whispered dreams and hearts so bold.
In corners dim, the laughter swells,
While silence weaves its magic spells.

A mirror's gaze reveals the truth,
Of fleeting moments, lost in youth.
With every glance, a story grows,
In gentle waves, the longing flows.

The walls absorb the secrets shared,
While flickering stars reveal they cared.
In echoes soft, the heart retrieves,
The light that lingers, never leaves.

And though the past may fade away,
In every heart, the echoes stay.
Reflections dance in pools of light,
A testament to love's sweet flight.

Crystals of the Night's Heart

In twilight's breath, the crystals gleam,
With every spark, the night will dream.
A tapestry of cosmic grace,
Where starlight finds its sacred place.

As shadows stretch and secrets plead,
The whispers weave through starlit seed.
With every twinkle, stories spun,
In the embrace of twilight's run.

The night holds treasures, veiled and bright,
With crystals glowing, purest light.
A tapestry of moments rare,
In silver threads, the dreams lay bare.

In quiet glades where silence sings,
The heart of night in beauty clings.
Each crystal's glow, a wish fulfilled,
In harmony, the void is thrilled.

So let the night, with secrets bold,
Reveal the wonders yet untold.
In crystals bright, the stories dart,
The twilight sings the night's dear heart.

Fractured Dreams of the Ethereal

In slumber's grasp where shadows tread,
Fractured dreams of moments fled.
With every pulse, the starlight breaks,
As slumber's veil slowly shakes.

The ethereal whispers call the night,
Guiding lost souls to silver light.
A realm where hopes and fears entwine,
In shards of dreams, the fates align.

Each shimmering piece, a story told,
Of broken vows and hearts of gold.
In whispers soft, the echoes swell,
In twilight's arms, all secrets dwell.

Yet from the splinters, beauty blooms,
In every heart, a spark resumes.
The light will shine through cracks so deep,
The fractured dreams begin to leap.

So let us dance in shadowed light,
Embrace the dreams that take their flight.
In fractured paths, our souls will soar,
Into the night, forevermore.

Echoing Laughter from the Abyss

In the depths where whispers loom,
A laughter dances, cloaked in gloom.
Echoes bounce off stony walls,
Revealing secrets as night falls.

Phantoms play in twilight's gleam,
And shadows stretch, like woven dreams.
A jester's voice, stark yet sweet,
Drawing hearts to anxious feet.

With every chuckle, a tale unwinds,
Of lost souls and wandering minds.
In laughter's grasp, they find their peace,
As the night draws close, their worries cease.

Yet heed the call from depths so dark,
For joy may wear a ghostly mark.
An echo here, a wisp of breath,
In the abyss, it flirts with death.

So laugh with care, and dance with light,
Amid the shadows, outright fright.
For in the echoes, wisdom lies,
A haunting truth beneath the skies.

Between Light and Shadow's Kiss

In the twilight where secrets blend,
Light and shadow twist and bend.
With every flicker, a promise made,
In whispers soft, the darkness played.

Dancing figures on dusky ground,
In the hush, lost dreams are found.
Moonlit tendrils reach with grace,
To touch the heart, to warm the space.

Beneath the stars, where wonders breathe,
A tranquil space, where spirits weave.
In twilight's arms, we find our way,
Through veils of night, to greet the day.

Yet linger not too long in shade,
For brighter truths are never stayed.
In shadows deep, we make our mark,
Between the light, we find the spark.

So let us dance on this fine line,
Where dreams awake and hearts align.
For in this realm of dusk's sweet bliss,
We live, we love, 'twixt light's soft kiss.

Tangles of the Dream Weaver

In a realm where dreams entwine,
The weaver spins in threads divine.
With colors bright and shadows pale,
She crafts the fate of each lost tale.

A flick of wrist, a flicker bright,
A tapestry in silver light.
Each strand a wish, a fear unfurled,
A glimpse into another world.

With careful hands, she guides the flow,
Of whispered hopes and silent woe.
In every knot, a story fast,
Of futures built and shadows cast.

Yet tangled dreams can lead astray,
When visions bend and stray away.
For every thread, a choice to make,
In woven paths, we dare to wake.

So trust the weaver's gentle art,
For she knows well the human heart.
In every tangle, wisdom lies,
In dreams, we soar, we learn to rise.

Each Flicker Holds a Secret

In twilight's glow, the stars appear,
Each flicker holds a tale, my dear.
Stories whispered in the night,
Of ancient wonders, lost to sight.

A lantern's breath, a wishful sigh,
Guides the dreamers passing by.
With every pulse, a truth reveals,
In soft illumination, the heart feels.

From shadows deep to starlit skies,
Each flicker holds the earth's goodbyes.
In glimmers small, the cosmos winks,
Inviting hearts to pause and think.

In every spark, behold the grace,
Of fleeting moments, time's embrace.
For in the dark, we learn to see,
The beauty wrapped in mystery.

So when the night begins to call,
Look to the flickers, one and all.
For every light, a softly spoken,
Secret yearning, love unbroken.

Whispers of Celestial Buttonholes

In shadows soft, the whispers tread,
Where buttonholes of stars are spread.
They wink and sigh in velvet night,
Holding secrets of pure delight.

With silver threads, our dreams entwined,
In skies where time is softly blind.
Each breath a wish, a silent prayer,
In cosmic dance beyond compare.

Through tangled mist, we seek the glow,
Of hidden paths the ancients know.
The laughter of the moonlight beams,
A guide to chart our silvery dreams.

Oh, realms where starlit tales unfold,
In buttonholes of mysteries told.
With every glance, our spirits soar,
To realms we've yearned for, evermore.

So listen close, the night will sing,
Of wondrous joys that dreams can bring.
The whispers weave a tapestry,
Of cosmic love, eternally.

Starlit Gaps in Mythical Dreams

In starlit gaps, where shadows play,
Mythical dreams come out to sway.
With every twinkle, secrets glean,
A world unseen, yet felt, serene.

Beneath the glow of ancient light,
Whispers beckon through the night.
Each dreamer's heart begins to soar,
As magic whispers evermore.

Time dances slow in silver streams,
Where hope alights and courage beams.
In myths we find our tales reborn,
Of heroes lost and legends worn.

With every wish cast to the sky,
We chase the swirls of stardust high.
In gaps of time, we dare to dream,
Our fantasies alight and gleam.

So gather close, let stories weave,
For in these gaps, we dare believe.
The night will cradle all we seek,
In mythical realms, our spirits speak.

Pockets of Light Beneath Enchantment

In pockets of light, enchantments dwell,
Where whispers of magic softly swell.
The flicker dances on the ground,
In gentle beams, sweet dreams are found.

Within the realm of fleeting rays,
The heart discovers hidden ways.
Each shimmering glint a guide to roam,
In pockets of light, we find our home.

The trees enchant with tales of old,
Of stardust dreams and legends told.
Underneath their boughs, we rest our fears,
As hope takes flight, dissolving tears.

With every breath, the night unfolds,
In pockets deep, our fate unfolds.
We gather starlight in our hands,
Creating worlds, as fate commands.

So let the glow ignite your soul,
For in the light, we're utterly whole.
In magical realms, both dark and bright,
We dance forever in pure delight.

Secrets of the Celestial Saddle

On celestial saddles, stars do ride,
With secrets whispered by the tide.
Each glimmer holds a tale untold,
Of cosmic wonders, bright and bold.

In twilight's grasp, the magic gleams,
Where starlit laughter spills through dreams.
The saddle cradles hopes anew,
As galaxies embrace the view.

With every wish, the night ignites,
In realms where joy and wonder bites.
To ride beyond the veils of fear,
In astral planes, our souls draw near.

Oh secrets shared on velvet night,
In celestial dances, pure delight.
We journey forth where shadows play,
In whispers soft that lead the way.

The saddle beckons, come take flight,
To explore the depth of starlit night.
With every pulse, a heartbeat sings,
As we embrace the joy it brings.

Patterns in the Hallowed Fabric

In whispers worn by ancient thread,
Patterns weave where dreams have fled.
Beneath the moon's soft, watchful gaze,
A tapestry of time displays.

Threads of gold and silver spun,
With tales of battles bravely won.
Each stitch an echo of a song,
Revealing where the hearts belong.

A needle's kiss, a seamstress' care,
In every fold, a magic rare.
The fabric hums with stories bold,
Of love and loss, both young and old.

A cloak of shadows, bright and deep,
Guarding secrets, dreams we keep.
In patterns formed, our lives collide,
In hallowed fabric, we abide.

Glimmers Through the Faerie Veil

In twilight's dance, the faeries play,
Glimmers bright lead lost souls astray.
With laughter like the summer rain,
They bring forth joy, dispel the pain.

Underneath the silver glaze,
Whispers weave in mystic ways.
A gentle hush, a secret told,
In glimmers soft, the night unfolds.

Through the veil, a shimmer glows,
Ancient mysteries that time bestows.
In dreams, we chase what's wondrous, free,
As faerie lights guide destiny.

Beneath the stars, our wishes blend,
In faerie realms, where rules suspend.
Each twinkle holds a promise bright,
A beacon in the endless night.

Caverns of Enigmatic Radiance

In caverns deep, where shadows dwell,
Enigmas hide, with tales to tell.
Diamonds spark in darkness grand,
Awakening the whispering land.

With echoing steps, we venture forth,
Into the heart of hidden worth.
Each stone a chronicle of time,
In radiant glow, a secret rhyme.

Crystals sing in colors rare,
Lighting paths with otherworldly flair.
In silence steeped, their wisdom flows,
Revealing what the darkness knows.

Through labyrinths, our spirits roam,
In radiant caverns, we find home.
In every glimmer, truth laid bare,
An invitation to venture there.

Echoes of the Charmed Fastening

In whispers soft as evening falls,
Echoes linger within the walls.
The charms we clasp, in silence bind,
Are stories lost, yet intertwined.

A fastening of fate and time,
In every click, a distant chime.
With every breath, a world awakes,
In echoes sweet, a promise makes.

Through corridors where shadows creep,
The charms we wear, their secrets keep.
In twilight's glow, reflections gleam,
Binding lives within a dream.

With every step, the heart can feel,
The magic woven into the reel.
In echoes past, the future calls,
In charmed fastenings, love enthralls.

Threads of Wonder in the Dark

In the stillness of the night,
Whispers weave through shadowed light.
Stars like secrets softly gleam,
Guiding wanderers through the dream.

With every flicker, tales unfold,
A tapestry of silence bold.
Each thread a story, faint but near,
In the dark, the wonders clear.

Footsteps echo on the ground,
Through the hidden paths unbound.
Magic swirls with every breath,
A dance of life that conquers death.

Around each corner, shadows play,
Dreamers linger, night turns day.
Within the quiet, softly hum,
The call of hearts that dare to come.

So let the midnight secrets sing,
Of journeys deep and daring things.
In threads of wonder, we embark,
Explorers bright, who chase the dark.

Secrets Etched in Cosmic Silence

In the void where stardust glows,
Ancient stories gently flow.
Whispers travel on the breeze,
Carried softly through the trees.

The cosmos hums with tales untold,
In shadows deep, the truths unfold.
Galaxies spin in silent dance,
Through time and space, they weave their trance.

Stars align in perfect array,
Guiding seekers on their way.
Each twinkle holds a hidden key,
Unlocking realms we yearn to see.

Between the beats of cosmic heart,
The universe plays its part.
In the silence, wisdom calls,
Upon the mind, the starlight falls.

So let us wander through the night,
Embrace the dark, seek out the light.
In secrets etched, our spirits rise,
To cosmic realms beyond the skies.

Journeys Beyond the Veil

Through the mist, the whispers guide,
Where the dreams and shadows bide.
Paths unseen and bridges cross,
In this realm, we gain and lose.

A silver thread, the light we trace,
In every heart, a hidden place.
With courage bold, we step ahead,
To chart the skies where few have tread.

Ghostly echoes murmur near,
Tales of both the far and dear.
In the twilight, courage swells,
For every soul, a story dwells.

Beyond the veil, the unknown waits,
With open arms and silent gates.
We dance with time, we chase the day,
In the space where dreams display.

So gather strength and keep your hope,
In the shadows, learn to cope.
For journeys far can lead us home,
In every heart, a place to roam.

The Dance of Unseen Wonders

In the dusk, where silence reigns,
Magic drips from moonlit veins.
Invisible hands weave and twirl,
In hidden worlds, the wonders swirl.

With every breath, a spirit sighs,
Painting dreams across the skies.
The dance of life, both fierce and free,
In shadows cast, it calls to thee.

Footsteps light on vibrant air,
Each heartbeat weaves a thread so rare.
Whirling stars in endless flight,
Embrace the echoes of the night.

Through gardens lost in time's embrace,
We find the joy of hidden grace.
The unseen wonders, soft and bright,
Awake the magic of the night.

So let us dance, let our hearts soar,
In every moment, seek for more.
In this ballet, forever spun,
The unseen wonders have begun.

Escape into the Realm of Shadows

In whispers soft where shadows creep,
The secrets of the night do seep,
A world beyond the sight of man,
Where dreams and dark in silence span.

Through veils of mist and silver gleam,
The heart's desires wake from dream,
With courage drawn from hidden depths,
We tread where light itself forgets.

The whispers call, a beckoning song,
To places where the lost belong,
With every breath, we learn to fly,
To dance beneath the starlit sky.

The shadows weave their timeless tale,
Of courage bold that will not pale,
In realms where most would fear to roam,
We find ourselves, and call it home.

So take my hand, embrace the night,
For in the dark, we find the light,
Together we shall brave the storm,
And in shadows, we are reborn.

Tales Told by the Silent Light

When twilight falls, the stars align,
In silence, truths begin to shine,
A gentle glow upon the earth,
Whispers of stories, long since birthed.

From shadows cast in tender gleams,
The night reveals its stitched-up seams,
Where echoes linger, tales unfold,
In glimmers bright, and heartbeats bold.

These tales of old, through ages span,
A dance of women, dreams of man,
With every flicker, paths collide,
In silent light, our hopes confide.

The moonlight bathes the weary soul,
As shimmering charges make us whole,
In whispered words, we find our place,
With silent light, we lose our haste.

So listen close, for time's embrace,
Holds stories in its sacred space,
In every ray, shadows ignite,
These tales unfold through silent light.

Grazing the Edges of Reality

In twilight's grasp, the worlds entwine,
Where dreams are drawn and stars align,
A dance that hovers on the edge,
Of truths that tease and softly pledge.

Through veils of thought that gently sway,
We tiptoe on the brink of day,
With visions bright, we fade and blend,
To realms where time and space transcend.

Each heartbeat carries whispers near,
Of stories held both faint and clear,
A tapestry of warped delight,
Grazing the edges, taking flight.

The horizon beckons, bright and bold,
In subtleties, the brave unfold,
With every breath, we journey forth,
Into the dreams that hold our worth.

So weave your thoughts and stretch your mind,
For in the fringe, all souls aligned,
Together we'll dance with all our might,
In grazing edges, we find our light.

The Thrum of Unseen Realities

In silence deep, the thrum resounds,
Where all the hidden truth abounds,
An undercurrent, soft yet strong,
A pulse of worlds where we belong.

The fabric woven, thread by thread,
In whispered tones, the stories spread,
From shadows born in twilight's glow,
The unseen paths that lie below.

Each heartbeat echoes in the void,
Awakening dreams that we've enjoyed,
With every breath, the layers peel,
Revealing what is truly real.

The thrum of time, the clockwork's flow,
In numbers veiled, the secrets show,
As realms collide in vibrant dance,
A cosmic waltz, a timeless chance.

So listen close, and heed the call,
For in the thrum, we rise or fall,
Embrace the unseen, set your sights,
In the thrum of life, we find our lights.

www.ingramcontent.com/pod-product-compliance
Ingram Content Group UK Ltd.
Pitfield, Milton Keynes, MK11 3LW, UK
UKHW021500280125
4335UKWH00035B/635